W9-AWK-501

The Black Hat Dances

Two Buddhist Boys in the Himalayas

The Black Hat Dances

Two Buddhist Boys in the Himalayas

Luree Miller

Photographs by Marilyn Silverstone

DODD, MEAD & COMPANY   *New York*

Text copyright © 1987 by Luree Miller
Photographs copyright © 1987 by Marilyn Silverstone
All rights reserved
No part of this book may be reproduced in any form without
permission in writing from the publisher
Distributed in Canada by
McClelland and Stewart Limited, Toronto
Manufactured in the United States of America

1   2   3   4   5   6   7   8   9   10

Library of Congress Cataloging-in-Publication Data

Miller, Luree.
    The black hat dances.

    Bibliography: p.
    Includes index.
    Summary: Describes the influence of their religious
beliefs on the lives of two Buddhist boys, one learning to
be a farmer, the other studying to be a monk, in the
Himalayan country of Sikkim. Includes information on the
history and basic principles of Buddhism.
    1. Buddhist children—India—Sikkim—Religious life
—Juvenile literature.   2. Buddhism—India—Sikkim—
Juvenile literature.   3. Sikkim (India)—Religious life
and customs—Juvenile literature.   [1. Buddhism—India—
Sikkim.   2. Sikkim (India)—Social life and customs]
I. Silverstone, Marilyn, ill.   II. Title.
BQ349.S57M55   1987   294.3'0954'167   87-540
ISBN 0-396-08835-X

CONTENTS

ACKNOWLEDGMENTS

I wish to thank Mr. Sonam T. Kazi for his great kindness in giving me his time and generous advice. To Brent Ashabranner, my gratitude for his invaluable counsel. Marilyn Silverstone and I are deeply indebted to the people of Sikkim who have welcomed us over the years and especially to the lamas and monks at Pemayangtse who helped make this book possible.

L.M.

The
Black Hat
Dances

Two Buddhist Boys in the Himalayas

The new Cambodian Buddhist temple near Washington, D.C. © *Luree Miller*

1

 BUDDHISM IN THE UNITED STATES

In a new house not far from the Capitol building in Washington, D.C., there is a large room with seven statues of the Buddha. A group of new Americans, who came from Cambodia, have made this house into their Buddhist temple.

A small Cambodian boy, about ten years old, slips through the doorway into the temple room. His name is Sarin. Shyly he joins about a dozen other Cambodian children who are standing quietly by the altar in front of the Buddha. They are waiting for their teacher.

This is the first time Sarin has come to the class on Buddhism. Nervously he wonders if the teacher will speak English. Already he has forgotten most of the prayers his mother taught him in Pali, the ancient language of Buddhism.

Sarin is a refugee. Like most of the Cambodians in the United States, his family fled from the fighting in their country. Before they could escape, Sarin's father was killed by the Khmer Rouge, a Communist faction of Cambodians. Sarin was a baby and hardly remembers how his mother carried him through the jungle to safety and finally to America. Sarin has gone to American schools since he was six and he wants to be like other American boys. But his mother does not want him to forget his religion. She works all day and cannot teach him herself. So she is very happy that at last a Buddhist monk from Cambodia has established the temple in Washington, D.C., and once a week will teach a class for children.

When the monk comes, Sarin is relieved to hear him speak to them in English. Before they begin their lessons, the monk says, they must pray to the Buddha. He assures them that when they learn to be good Buddhists, no matter what happens to them, they will be strong enough to stand by themselves. Sarin glances up at the serene smiling face of the great Buddha at the center of the altar. A tingle of joy and strength shoots down his spine. He places the palms of his hands together and raises them to his forehead. With the rest of the children he begins to chant in Pali. He has not forgotten his prayers after all.

Buddhism is one of the world's great religions, with over 500 million followers. Many Americans do not realize that today it is a growing religion in the United States. It is the major religious denomination of the state of Hawaii. Nobody knows exactly how many Americans consider themselves Buddhists, but certainly there are hundreds of thousands. Many forms of Buddhism are practiced and these different sects do not keep records of the numbers in their congregations the way Jews and Christians do.

A statue of the Buddha. When he became Enlightened, he touched the earth with his right hand.
© *Luree Miller*

A Tibetan religious painting on cloth is called a *thanka*. © *Arlene Blum*

Buddhism began more than twenty-five centuries ago with a man who was born in India, on the border of Nepal. He was a prince named Siddhartha. He became such a great teacher that people gave him the title "the Buddha," which, in Sanskrit, the classical language of ancient India, means "The Enlightened One." The Buddha taught that the world is full of suffering and that every type of suffering has a particular cause. Everything each person does has either a good or bad effect. Their thoughts and actions affect not only others, but more important, determine what will happen to themselves. This is what Buddhists call *karma*. Karma is the result of our own actions.

Therefore every human being has a personal responsibility to avoid evil thoughts and actions, to learn good ways to think and act, and to try to eliminate the causes of suffering. By adhering to what the Buddha called The Middle Way of reason and meditation, people can learn to be compassionate and to live in harmony with themselves and with the whole world.

The Buddha explained that life moves on a never-ending wheel of birth, death, and rebirth. Every living being has had a previous life and will be reborn in another form of life. So all forms of life are related to each other, from human beings to the tiniest ants. The Buddha called every creature with the spark of life a *sentient* being. He taught compassion for all sentient beings, who, like ourselves, wish for happiness and do not want to suffer. Therefore, he said, people should practice compassion and nonviolence and cherish every form of life.

Buddhism spread throughout Asia to Sri Lanka, Burma, Thailand, Laos, Cambodia, Vietnam, Tibet, China, Korea, and Japan. In every country it developed some different traditions and practices. Chinese Buddhism has some rituals different from Cambodian Buddhism. Tibetan Buddhism is in some ways different from the Buddhism practiced in Japan. But the basic religious philosophy is the same for all Buddhists everywhere.

Japanese settlers on the West Coast of the United States were the first to build Buddhist temples in this country. That was nearly ninety years ago. Today their children's children's children are still Buddhists. Billy and Amy Tanaka's great grandparents came to Seattle from Japan in 1900. They belonged to a Buddhist sect called Jodoshin-Shu, which means "True School of the Pure Land." The next year, in 1901, they helped establish the Seattle Buddhist Church.

Now Billy and Amy go with their parents to the Buddhist church. It is on a steep hill across from a playground. Sometimes, when the sun is shining, they play with their friends on the playground until the church service is over. Their parents know that it is hard for wiggly children to sit still on the hard wooden pews while the priest gives his sermon.

But after the service Billy and Amy always go to Sunday school. They sit on chairs in a small meeting room while their teacher tells them wonderful stories about the Buddha's life.

Once Billy told Amy that even though he likes playing baseball at the playground, he likes going to the church service with the grown-ups too. He likes the solemn feeling he has when he puts his hands together before his forehead, bows his head and chants, with the whole congregation, the prayer that opens the service, *Namo amida butsu.* It means, "I bow to the Buddha of Boundless Light." This prayer is the only Japanese used in the service or in Sunday school and is the only Japanese Billy and Amy ever speak.

Amy agrees with Billy. There are always flowers in front of the Buddha and sometimes she brings a sprig of lilac or a branch of cherry blossoms for the altar. Then Amy feels as if the Buddha smiles especially for her.

The Seattle Buddhist Church in Seattle, Washington. © *Stephanie Smith*

A Tibetan trumpet. The Tibetan Buddhist Center, Berkeley, California. © *Arlene Blum*

But Asian-Americans are not the only Buddhists in the United States. There also are non-Oriental Americans who decide to join the Buddhist religion. Sometimes they learn about it when they travel to Japan, China, India, or Nepal. Sometimes they read a book or see a picture or meet a person in the United States who teaches them about Buddhism.

When the Dalai Lama, who is the spiritual head of Tibetan Buddhism, left Tibet in 1959 because Chinese troops occupied his country, many monks came with him. They brought their holy books and built new monasteries in India and Nepal and in European countries and the United States. Since then other Tibetans have come to live in countries all over the world. The Dalai Lama stayed in the Himalayan foothills of India where he now lives with many of his followers at a place called Dharamsala.

Pema's mother and father met in Berkeley, California. Her mother had always lived in Berkeley but her father came from Tibet. When Pema was born they decided to give her a Tibetan name. When she was old enough, they began taking her to the Tibetan Buddhist Center so that she would learn about her father's religion.

Now Pema is eleven and she looks forward to the Sundays she and her mother and father go to the Center. It is in a big house perched on a high hill overlooking the ocean. When she goes there, Pema pretends she is on a mountain peak above a green valley in the Himalayan Mountains where there are the Tibetan Buddhist monasteries her father has told her about. Beside the walk leading to the Tibetan Buddhist Center there are strings of white flags printed with Tibetan prayers. The flags flutter in the wind, sending their prayers up to the heavens, the way they do around the Buddhist monasteries.

Inside the Center are little prayer rugs on round cushions scattered across the floor to sit on. Pema searches for her favorite rug with a blue dragon design. Then she settles down on it in the traditional cross-legged position like the statue of the Buddha that she faces. Everyone around her is quiet. Pema closes her eyes and tries to imagine the whole world with its wide oceans and the giant Himalayan Mountains where her father came from.

A wonderful feeling of being friends with all sentient beings—all living creatures—wherever they are, wells up in her. Silently she says to herself the ancient Buddhist prayer:

> May all beings have happiness and the cause of happiness.
> May they be free from suffering and the cause of suffering.
> May they be inseparable from the happiness which is without
> suffering,
> Separated from the extremes of far and near, attachment and
> aversion.
> May they dwell in boundless equanimity.

Pema's prayer is the same one said by all Tibetan Buddhists everywhere. Half a world away, in India, at the foot of the Himalayas, this prayer is repeated daily by two boys Pema's age. Their names are Tashi and Samdup.

2

 TWO BUDDHIST BOYS IN SIKKIM

Nestled in the shadow of the highest mountains in the world is Sikkim, in the northeast corner of India. This is where Samdup and Tashi live. Sikkim is a place of magical beauty. The forests are filled with birds and butterflies bright as jewels. Orchids twine themselves along the branches of the trees. Terraced fields of rice are watered by delicate bamboo aqueducts dripping water from field to field down the hillsides. The fragrance from orange groves and fields of the sweet spice, cardamom, floats on the clear mountain air. Children play under Buddhist prayer flags fluttering in the wind.

When Samdup and Tashi look up, they see the great Himalayan Mountain range. The snowy peaks fill the entire horizon as far as the eye can see. They are dazzling white against a deep blue sky. Some peaks are more than five miles high.

11

Clouds rising to cover the peaks of Kanchenjunga.

The Himalayas form a border 1,600 miles long that separates the subcontinent of India from the high plateau of Tibet. To Buddhists in India, Nepal, Bhutan, and Tibet, the Himalayas are sacred mountains. They are sacred also to the followers of the Hindu religion in India and Nepal.

For over a hundred years, mountaineers have beeen drawn by the challenge of climbing the Himalayan Mountains. In 1955 a British expedition climbed the Himalayan peak of Kanchenjunga, the third highest mountain in the world. Kanchenjunga is the name of the deity who is the guardian of the upper valley of Sikkim. Out of respect to this divinity, who resides on the summit, the British climbers stopped a few feet from the top of the mountain.

To Samdup and Tashi, Kanchenjunga is a powerful protector, one of the many guardians of their religion in Sikkim. Tashi lives with his family on a small farm. It is on the side of a steep foothill facing Kanchenjunga. Samdup lives in the Buddhist monastery at the top of the hill. The monastery is called Pemayangtse.

Samdup and Tashi are good friends. Under the watchful protection of Kanchenjunga, they have played together since they were very small. But Tashi is a farm boy and Samdup is studying to become a monk. They are growing and changing and beginning to see how different their lives will be.

The older Samdup gets, the more responsibilities he has. He knows that if he studies hard and passes his examinations he will become a full-fledged Buddhist monk. He will spend the rest of his life living very much like monks have lived for thousands of years: studying, saying prayers, performing rituals, and striving for greater spiritual knowledge. But sometimes so much studying and being with his teachers seem like a heavy load to Samdup. There are times when he envies the freedom Tashi has being outdoors helping with the farm work and looking after the animals.

Tashi.   Samdup.

Pemayangtse monastery at the top of the hill above the village of Gayshing.

Tashi watches a small student monk hurrying to join the others inside
the monastery.

Tashi does not know what the future holds for him. From listening to his parents and their friends, he understands that life in India is changing. It is becoming harder to make a living from a small family farm. Besides he is not sure that he wants to be a farmer like his father.

Now Samdup is busy helping the older monks get ready for a festival at Pemayangtse. When Tashi climbs up the hill to the monastery, Samdup has no time to play. As Tashi watches Samdup and all the other students in their warm maroon robes and long scarves hurrying inside the monastery to take their places beside the monks, he often feels left out and alone. Then he is jealous of Samdup in his secure world.

Other times, when the mist rises up from the deep valleys and the snow-chilled wind tingles his cheeks, Tashi feels stirring in him the blood of his nomadic ancestors who herded yaks in the high Himalayas. Then he has an urge to climb up the trails leading out of his village to see for himself what lies over the mountains.

3

 TASHI LIVES ON A SMALL FARM

Tashi is eleven years old. He has bright black eyes and a sparkling smile. Like most of the people who live in the Himalayan foothills, Tashi is small but very strong from climbing and carrying loads up and down the hills.

Tashi lives with his mother, father, older brother, and little sister on a small farm a short walk up the hill from a village named Gayshing. The farm is five acres of fields terraced one above the other. In these steep hills, farmers must build terraces to make level plots of land for their crops. One year Tashi's father, Norbu, plants his fields in rice and millet and the next year in wheat and corn. All along the vast sweep of the Himalayas, the hillsides are terraced in small farms like Norbu's.

Tashi's house. He is bringing a kettle of water for his mother to make tea.

When the morning sun comes up it lights the five-pointed peak of Kanchenjunga a rosy pink. Then the sunlight spreads down the mountainside to the foothills, lighting the monastery at the top of the hill, then Tashi's farm and finally, the village of Gayshing. Every morning the first sound to break the still dawn air is a rooster crowing. Its loud confident crow awakens Tashi. Soon the cold morning air is full of animal sounds: cows mooing, pigs grunting, donkeys braying, sheep and goats bleating, and village dogs barking.

Tashi's family owns two goats and a kid, three cows and a calf, four pigs and six piglets, one rooster and eight chickens, and a big golden woolly dog named Tag-Toog. Tag-Toog means tiger cub, which is what Tag-Toog looked like when he was a puppy.

At night the animals are kept in the bottom half of the house. It is made of stone and has stalls and a dirt floor covered with straw. The second floor of the house is wooden with glass-paned windows that open out like shutters. The family lives in two big rooms in this upper half of the house. But most of the time they are working outside in the fields and farmyard, except during the rainy season. Then, for three months, everybody spends more time indoors. There is a steady drumming of raindrops on the tin roof and a musty smell of wet clothes drying by the charcoal fire in the stone hearth.

Among many Buddhist families it is a tradition for the firstborn son to become a monk. Palden, Tashi's older brother, was taken by his father to the monastery at the top of the hill, when he was seven years old, to begin his studies. So it is Tashi, the younger brother, who helps on the farm and looks after the animals. His little sister. Chöny, helps her mother with cooking, cleaning, and weeding in the fields. Tashi calls his mother *Ama* and his father *Aba*.

"Where is the water for tea?" Tashi's mother calls to him. "I hear you, Ama," Tashi replies as he rolls out of his blanket and pulls on his heavy cotton shirt and pants. He grabs the big teakettle and

scrambles down the notched log that leads from the back porch to the narrow ledge of ground behind the house. The path from the house to the river is so straight downhill that as Tashi runs, his bare feet send showers of pebbles pelting down ahead of him. By the time he climbs back up with the teakettle full of water he is very hungry. But Ama is waiting with a pan of mash for Tashi to feed to the pigs. Smiling gently, she hands it to him.

Ama's name is Dechen. Her father is a farmer in a village a day's walk from Gayshing. When she was fourteen, Dechen's parents looked for a husband for her. Dechen was happy with their selection of Norbu because he is a good farmer and a loving husband and father. Daily she thanks the Buddha for her good fortune. Whenever she has a spare moment she says her prayers and twirls her prayer wheel, a round box that turns on a short handle. Inside the prayer wheel are many prayers printed on rice paper. Buddhists believe very strongly in the power of prayers. They believe prayers do not have to be said to be heard, that turning prayer wheels sets the prayers inside them in motion which is beneficial to all the world. But saying prayers at the same time is even better, so all day as they go about their work, the people of the Himalayas murmur *"Om Mani Padme Hum,"* "Oh, Jewel in the Lotus," to the Buddha of Mercy or Compassion.

Around her left wrist Dechen wears a rosary of 108 beads for counting her prayers. Around her neck she wears a silver box, called a *gao*. The *gao* is filled with prayers and precious relics blessed by a lama. Tashi wears his small silver prayer holder on a cord around his upper arm and he hums *Om Mani Padme Hum* like a favorite tune.

Humming, he jumps up on the stone wall in front of his house and walks along it balancing the heavy pan of food for the pigs. By now the sun is higher and has pushed back the cold shadows that made Tashi shiver in the early morning. The sunshine feels deli-

Tashi calls his mother Ama.

The pigs grunt hungrily as Tashi pours their food into the feeding trough. The calf watches.

ciously warm on his back. A sweet smell of manure and damp straw fills the air. Already Dechen and Chöny have swept the farmyard. The chickens and rooster strut about, all puffed up in the extra fluff of feathers which have grown to protect them from the cold weather. When the pigs hear Tashi coming, they grunt and come trotting as fast as they can on their short legs to the food trough where Tashi pours out their meal. With their mud-brown snouts and long black bristles, they look very much like wild boars.

All the animals are so eager to eat it makes Tashi laugh. He knows just how they feel. His own stomach is rattling. He feeds the cows an armful of stiff yellow mustard stalks. They roll their big brown eyes at him and wag their ears. The calf runs in circles, making Tashi laugh even harder as he pulls the rope to tie her to a tree so she won't drink her mother's milk. She is getting too big for milk and Dechen will use the cow's milk for the family.

Tashi clicks his tongue and scatters grain on the ground for the chickens. Then he notices that the little kid is not with the two goats busily nibbling leaves from the thick bushes that grow above his house. Quickly Tashi scrambles up the hill and finds the kid caught in a tangle of vines. Tashi tears away the vines and swoops the squirming kid up in his arms. It bleats loudly as he carries it back down the hill.

Sometimes looking for a kid or calf that has strayed makes Tashi late for school. But he enjoys taking care of the animals. They are his friends. He talks to them and knows they understand, particularly Tag-Toog, the family's old dog that likes to lie in the sun. Tag-Toog wags his tail when he sees Tashi coming. Tashi pats him on the shoulder and Tag-Toog lifts up his paw to shake hands.

Back at his house Tashi gulps down a cup of hot tea flavored with salt and butter and eats a handful of rice popped like Rice Krispies. Then he runs down the hill to school, past the terraces

25

The calf runs in circles when Tashi ropes it.

below the farmyard where the wheat in Aba's fields is green tipped with gold. Prayer flags flapping softly on tall bamboo poles surround the fields. As Tashi nears Gayshing, he hears a sound as old as history—the murmur of voices from a village market. Merchants call out for people to come and buy their goods, customers bargain over prices, friends meet, talking and laughing. A village market, held one or two days a week, is a time-honored tradition in all of Asia and much of Europe.

Tashi always is eager to see if there is anything new for sale on market day. He cuts across the market square walled by a bazaar of wooden shops. The fruit and vegetable sellers are sitting out in the sunshine instead of under the long tin roof that runs down the middle of the marketplace. Tashi picks his way around mounds of red chilis, black tea leaves, big green cabbages, purple onions, and long yellow yams.

As he skips between some open sacks of rice, a woman with a wrinkled face calls out, "What news does this schoolboy bring us old grainsellers?"

"Ah, Grandma." Tashi grins. "No news. School is the same. My head is so stuffed with learning it will split like your sack of rice." He pokes his finger in a hole in her sack where the rice is spilling out.

The old woman slaps at him, chuckling, "Meddlers like you will be reborn a rat."

Tashi hurries on so she can't tease him anymore. In the middle of the market he stops to look at a stack of red T-shirts with pictures of motorcycles stenciled on them. Then he has to run so he won't be late for his first class. In school Tashi has classes in science, mathematics, geography, social studies, Sikkimese, English, and Hindi, the official language of India. He likes learning languages. At home he speaks Sikkimese but in the bazaar he hears a mixture of the many

The woman selling tea leaves in the market teases Tashi.

languages spoken in the Himalayas. He has learned words and phrases from merchants who speak Tibetan, Nepalese, or Urdu and he can carry on a conversation in Tsong, the language of a small group of Sikkimese.

When Tashi crosses the market ground again in the afternoon, on his way home from school, it is empty. The merchants have packed up their goods and gone. A hum of sewing machines coming from some of the open-fronted shops is the only sound. He hurries up the hill to home where Ama has a pot of chicken boiling over the fire. Tashi sits cross-legged on a mat with his father to eat his evening meal. Ama and Chöny must wait until the men are finished before they can eat. But they all chatter, telling each other what has happened during the day.

Tashi likes to tease Chöny because she always believes him and looks so scared. "In the forest I heard a ghost saying your name," Tashi tells her. "Listen, I can hear him outside now." Chöny looks anxiously over her shoulder and edges closer to the fire. "Nothing follows you but your black or white deeds," says Aba.

While there is still enough light to read by, Tashi takes his book to study on the stone wall. The valley below is filled with fluffy clouds and from the next farm comes the soft cooing of pet pigeons. Sitting on the wall, Tashi has trouble keeping his eyes open to read his book. After the day's work he is tired. He thinks how easy it must be for Samdup to do nothing but study and never have to feed the animals or carry water.

When the sun disappears over the edge of the Himalayas, little fires at farms all across the hills light up like fireflies in the darkness. There is no electricity and kerosine lamps make pools of light in the dark rooms of the farmhouses.

Inside his own snug house, Tashi says his evening prayers. He watches his mother prepare the family altar for the night. She care-

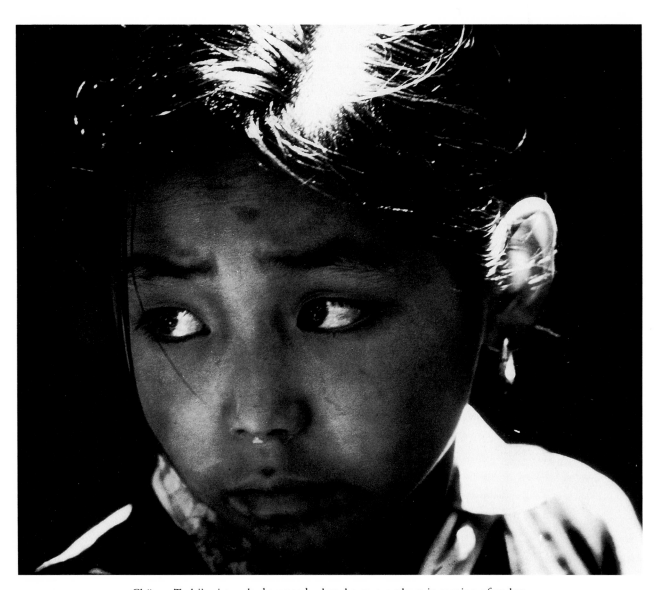

Chöny, Tashi's sister, looks scared when he says a ghost is coming after her.

fully empties the traditional seven bowls of water that are placed on the altar each morning. She wipes the bowls dry and turns them upside down. Clean water signifies purity, so the bowls must be refilled each day. Then she lights a small lamp of liquid butter, like a candle lighted on an altar in a church or synagogue. The day is done and Tashi rolls up in a warm wool blanket on his straw sleeping mat. At the very top of the window he glimpses the stars strung out above the dark peaks of Kanchenjunga. Then he falls sound asleep in the deep stillness of the mountain night.

The temple at Pemayangtse.

4

 SAMDUP LIVES IN A MONASTERY

The monastery at the top of the hill is called Pemayangtse. When Samdup was seven years old his parents brought him to Pemayangtse where he was accepted as a novice or student. Samdup is his monk's name. It was given to him when he took his vows in a special ceremony for novices entering the monastery. He also was given a new maroon robe like monks wear.

At Pemayangtse the monks belong to the Nyingmapa sect. The Nyingmapa is the oldest sect of Tibetan Buddhism. Sometimes they are called Red Hats because of the color of their hats.

At first Samdup missed his mother and father and brothers and sisters very much. But Pemayangtse is a friendly place where everyone feels welcome. Children of families who help support the mon-

Two young monks in their red hats blow conch shells.

astery play behind the temple. Samdup saw two little girls rolling a wooden wheel like a hoop the way his sisters did. He heard babies gurgling and laughing. The children made him feel more at home, yet lonely too for his own family.

Among the eight novices were three little boys younger than Samdup. Several boys were his own age and some, like Tashi's brother, Palden, were older. In a while Samdup felt as if these families, and the monks and novices who live in the monks' quarters, and those who live in nearby villages and come to Pemayangtse every day, were his own new family.

From that time Samdup, who now is eleven, has lived at Pemayangtse. At Pemayangtse, as in other Sikkimese monasteries, there are both monks and married priests. Both join in the work of the monastery. Samdup's teacher is his grandfather, Pema Chopel, a married priest. Samdup's parents are farmers and live a day's walk from Pemayangtse. When they come to see him they bring offerings of butter for the butter lamps at the monastery and corn for the monks.

Monasteries are sanctuaries for study and meditation and occasional ceremonies. Buddhist monasteries in the Himalayas are built on the tops of hills or on rocky mountain ledges and are called *Gonpas*. The word *Gonpa* means "A Dwelling in the Solitude." The Pemayangtse *Gonpa* sits on the summit of an Himalayan foothill 7,000 feet high. It is higher than most mountains in the United States.

The buildings at Pemayangtse have brown wooden shutters to close when the winds blow down from the Himalayan snows. The cold winds whistle through the oak and chestnut trees and topple the pots of red geraniums standing by the doors. At the very highest point of the hill, above the huts where the servants for the monastery live, and higher than the long wooden monks' quarters and the seven stone houses for the senior monks, is the large temple where religious services are held. The temple is a big white building with a broad

35

chocolate-colored band painted around it and a shining tin roof trimmed in yellow carved woodwork.

Early every morning, long before the sun rises, Samdup gets up in the darkness. He rolls up his quilted mat on the wooden platform where he sleeps in the monks' quarters with four other novices. The boys yawn and stretch and sometimes grumble about how early it is or how cold. "Hurry," Samdup says, *"Cho-Trimpa* will whack us if we are late."* The Cho-Trimpa is the monk in charge of keeping order in the monastery. Even though Samdup is a responsible novice and takes his duties very seriously, he worries that he will do something wrong and Cho-Trimpa will thump him with his stick.

The boys run barefoot across the big courtyard and up the stone stairs to the temple for morning prayers. Prayer flags surrounding the big white building flutter softly, sending messages on the wind to the guardian deities on the summits of the Himalayas. At the doorway of the temple, the Kings of the Four Quarters are painted on the walls. The Four Quarters are north, south, east, and west. The Four Kings guard these quarters of the universe and the heavens against Outer Demons.

Samdup hurries into the temple to take his place with the novices and monks. They all sit cross-legged on the two long wooden benches that face each other at right angles to the altar. The Abbot or *Rin-poche* is in his seat and the morning service has already begun. The Rinpoche is a lama. Many people call all Tibetan monks lamas, but that is not correct. A lama is a high authority in the Tibetan Buddhist religious community and a great teacher or the reincarnation of a great teacher. Not all Tibetan Buddhist monks are lamas.

The Rinpoche sits on a high seat near the altar reading from a holy book on a stand in front of him. With a brass thunderbolt scepter in his right hand and a bell in his left hand, he presides over the service. Samdup always feels a deep happiness when he hears the

Mist-covered mountains and prayer flags surround Pemayangtse.

Monks play trumpets and beat the drums during religious services inside the temple.

sweet note of the Rinpoche's bell and watches his hands making the graceful gestures of the ancient Buddhist ritual. Every gesture has a special meaning in the service.

On the bench opposite him are the monks who play the cymbals, blow the trumpets, and beat the goatskin drums. At the proper time Samdup chants his prayers with the other novices. But he notices that two of the small boys have nodded and fallen asleep. Others are squirming and peering over their shoulders for the servant who brings them morning tea. Samdup glances out of the corner of his eyes at Cho-Trimpa to see if he knows that some of the novices are not paying attention. Cho-Trimpa sits on a special bench higher than the novices (but not as high as the Rinpoche). He scowls and Samdup quickly looks away.

When a servant passes down the line and pours him his tea, Samdup cups the warm bowl in his hands and sips the hot tea, feeling its delicious warmth all the way down to his stomach. It is dawn. Pale light from the small windows near the ceiling falls on the altar. Now Samdup can see the giant image of Guru Padma Sambhava, the Buddhist saint and teacher who brought the teachings of the Buddha to Tibet. Guru Padma Sambhava is gilded all over with gold. Before him stand seven bowls of holy water. Rows of copper lamps filled with clear liquid butter and cotton wicks burn with small flames in front of Guru Padma Sambhava. Sticks of incense send thin swirls of spicy-smelling smoke clouding up beneath the brightly colored silk banners hanging from the ceiling.

Buddhists believe that concentrating on images helps train the mind to stop the flow of evil thoughts. As the Dalai Lama explains, "An undisciplined mind expresses evil thoughts by evil actions." For this reason, there are many figures of deities in Tibetan Buddhism. Some are fierce and terrible looking to overcome obstacles. Some are serene and peaceful to make the mind feel calm and compassionate.

39

Samdup has to concentrate very hard to follow the service. On his lap he has a stack of loose pages of rice paper printed with the prayers he is learning to memorize. But sometimes, when he is studying, Samdup can't help thinking about the way he used to run in the fields and build rock dams in the stream by his house.

Finally there is a break in the morning service. Samdup has been sitting so long he is stiff when he stands up. With the other novices he crowds out through the great wooden doors and down the steps of the temple. Together the boys race into the courtyard to stretch their legs. Then, after a short break, Cho-Trimpa's gong calls them back to prayers.

Late in the morning Samdup hears the servants carrying the big brass kettle full of boiled rice onto the porch of the temple. It is time for the first meal of the day. Eagerly he lines up with the novices on the porch. Each boy cups his hands together to receive from a servant a large leaf for a plate. As they troop by the kettle, another servant scoops a helping of rice onto each one's leaf. The novices serve the rice to the monks still seated in the temple. Then they return for their own servings.

In the afternoon, Samdup is free to play with Tashi and his other friends. He is glad to be outside. But by four o'clock he has to return to his room to study the prayers he must memorize to recite by heart. He and the other novices shout out their prayers because that helps them to remember.

Then Samdup goes to Pema Chopel and gives him the pages he has been studying. He sits cross-legged on the ground in front of his teacher to recite what he has learned. Samdup always worries that he will stutter and make a mistake. If he does, Pema Chopel gives him a stinging flick on the forehead with his bamboo stick.

After his evening meal at six o'clock, Samdup returns to the temple with the other novices and monks for prayers. As he says his

A novice steals a glance at Cho-Trimpa, the monk who keeps order, as they all take a break from the service to eat and drink tea.

A novice receives his rice.

prayers, Samdup shows his respect for the Buddha by pressing his hands together to touch his forehead, then his throat and his chest. He kneels and bows so that his hands, knees, and forehead touch the ground. He repeats this again and again, all the while murmuring *Om Mani Padme Hum* and other prayers.

Another more difficult religious exercise he practices is stretching flat out, face down on the ground, and pressing his hands together in front of the top of his head, then standing up and going down on the ground again and again. By this, he demonstrates his devotion to the Buddha and to his teachings. For every speck of dust that his two knees, two hands, and forehead touch, a bad deed of the past is cancelled out.

When there is a religious festival to prepare for, Samdup has little time to play. In the afternoon he must help the monks. Today he goes to the temple to knead a mixture of boiled rice and butter for *torma.* Pema Chopel molds the mixture into conelike offerings to be used in the Black Hat Dances that will be performed at Pemayangtse's yearly festival. Pema Chopel also makes an image that will capture all the evil spirits that must be destroyed to rid the world of sin and disaster.

Samdup kneels on the floor with his sleeves rolled up, kneading the dough in a big flat tray. He knows it is an important job. He has to get the mixture just right so it will hold its shape. He works fast to keep up with his grandfather who rolls the dough and shapes it with sure, swift hands. But while Samdup works, he can't help wishing he were outside with Tashi watching the crowds of people and pack trains of ponies coming into Gayshing for the fair and the Black Hat and other religious dances at Pemayangtse.

Buddhist festivals are great events and even the littlest novices

Samdup kneads a mixture of boiled rice and butter for his grandfather to mold into offerings called *torma*.

A small novice in ceremonial dress swings an incense burner.

A novice preparing to sprinkle holy water on the *torma*.

take part in the ceremonies. They wear their peaked red hats and each one has something special to do. The novice who swings the incense burner is allowed to wear a beautiful brocade cloth over his robe. Another novice sprinkles the *tormas* with holy water from a pot with grass and a peacock feather top, whenever an offering has to be purified.

Samdup is particularly excited, and a little bit scared too, because in this year's ceremonies he will be serving the powerful old lama who will perform the chief Black Hat Dance. This special dance can be done only by a most powerful lama whose concentration and recitation of special prayers is so strong he can overcome the forces of evil.

This lama lives in one of the houses behind the temple. After Samdup has finished helping Pema Chopel, he runs past the house hunting for Tashi. Just then the lama flings open his shutters. Samdup stops and looks up anxiously. The old lama leans out the window and peers down at Samdup. Then he slowly raises his hand from the windowsill. The gesture is small. But it signifies acceptance. Samdup races down the hill to tell Tashi that the powerful lama has given him a sign of approval.

Looking out the window of his house, the powerful lama raises his hand in a small gesture to Samdup.

Tashi carries wood to earn money.

5

 THE FAIR AT PEMAYANGTSE

Tashi is always looking for ways to earn money. He sells milk, eggs, or vegetables for his farm neighbors who are too busy to take their produce to the village. He carries bundles of firewood from the forest for the shopkeepers. When there is a festival such as the Black Hat Dances at Pemayangtse, there are many more jobs for Tashi to do.

Tashi is proud that his earnings help the family to buy sugar, salt, seeds for planting, and the few other things they purchase at the market in Gayshing. Even though Norbu is a good farmer, he must do other work to make enough money for the family to live. Norbu earns a small amount as a caretaker at Pemayangtse, making sure there is enough wood for the monks' cooking and heating. Sometimes he plows another farmer's field or looks after someone else's animals.

Everyone in the family works hard. Dechen and Chöny spend long hours collecting firewood. But the forests of the Himalayan foothills are being cut down so rapidly that they have to walk farther and farther from their farm to find enough wood. Dechen and Norbu worry about what will happen to their fields if too many trees on the hill above them are cut down. Tree roots help hold the soil in place when the heavy rains of the monsoon season beat down on the Himalayan foothills. Already Norbu and Dechen have seen fields turned to mud and washed down the mountains by flooding rains.

"What will happen to us if our fields slip down the mountain? How will Tashi take care of us if he has no farm?" Dechen asked Norbu. In Buddhist cultures it is traditional for children to feed, clothe, and look after their parents when they are old.

"Maybe Tashi should go away to school in Gangtok where he can learn mechanics or some trade that will prepare him to take a job," Norbu answers. Gangtok is the capital of Sikkim. It is more than fifty miles from Gayshing.

Dechen looks up at the mountains. "Gangtok is so far away," she says.

When the merchants begin arriving for the festival at Pemayangtse, Tashi and his friend Palchen meet by a tree along the road winding down into Gayshing. Around the bend come Moslem merchants with turbans carrying tin trunks on their heads. Tall Tibetans with black pigtails down their backs and big lumpy sacks slung over their shoulders stride past them. Nepalese traders lead pack ponies with bells around their necks and plumes of red-dyed yak tails tied to their halters. Tashi counts seventeen sturdy little ponies. With growing excitement, he wonders what is in the sacks strapped on their backs. Some ponies are loaded with upturned tables and benches and rolls of bamboo matting for the merchants to set up their stalls at Pemayangtse.

Tashi and his friend Palchen meet on the road to Gayshing.

Water in a five-gallon can is a heavy load for Tashi to carry.

Tashi and his friend Palchen meet on the road to Gayshing.

Water in a five-gallon can is a heavy load for Tashi to carry.

"Hey, you boys with nothing to do," a merchant calls out to Tashi and Palchen. "I need water for my tea stall."

"We will bring it," they shout happily. All that morning Tashi, Palchen, and their friends carry loads of water and armloads of firewood up the trail to the merchants setting up the fair at Pemayangtse. They carry the water in five-gallon kerosene cans, one at a time, on their backs. They carry the cans the way heavy loads are carried in the Himalayas—with a long wide cloth strap that is tied around the forehead, down over the shoulders, and under or around whatever is carried on a person's back. *Om Mani Padme Hum,* Tashi murmurs as he trudges up the trail with a heavy can of water on his back. Like all Buddhists, he takes every opportunity to pray, even as he works.

"Do you want to play *koppe?*" Tashi asks his friends when he is too tired to carry any more loads. They agree and with a stick Tashi digs a hole in the ground the size of an egg. About ten paces from the hole, the boys line up. The game is to toss a coin into the hole. Whoever flips his coin directly in gets to keep the coins that have already been tossed and are lying on the ground. Tashi wishes Samdup could play with them. His favorite game is when the novices and the farm boys flip coins across the ditch running around the temple. But now Samdup is in the temple helping the monks prepare for the festival.

Suddenly Tashi hears something. "Listen!" he hisses. The boys freeze. The sound of a jeep shifting gears echoes between the hillsides. They scoop up their coins and run as fast as they can into Gayshing. Just as they reach the bazaar, a canvas-topped jeep barrels to a stop in the marketplace. Out jumps the driver. He is Tenzing, the young agricultural development officer, who comes every month to help farmers like Norbu with new seeds and fertilizers and better methods of farming.

53

Tossing coins is a favorite game of Tashi and his friends.

Picking up the coins.

Ready for the jeep ride.

Palchen and Tashi have a serious talk.

"Will you give us a ride, Tenzing?" Tashi asks.

"Climb in," Tenzing says. The boys clamber up over the spare tire into the back end of the jeep. Tenzing revs the engine, lets out the clutch, and the jeep lurches forward. They speed up the switchback out of Gayshing. Tashi hangs out the back watching the tires send showers of small stones over the sheer side of the mountain. He likes the feeling of flying past fields and orchards and wishes they could keep going right up Kanchenjunga.

After their ride, Tashi and Palchen sit in the jeep to talk.

"Maybe I will become a jeep driver," says Tashi.

"Not me." says Palchen.

"Why not?"

"Because," Palchen declares, "You have to go away from Gayshing to a school in Gangtok. There are many things to learn."

"But that is what Samdup had to do. He had to leave his family and go to Pemayangtse to learn to be a monk," Tashi answers.

"Every monk has a full rice bowl," says Palchen. "Who knows how often a jeep driver eats?"

Tashi doesn't argue with Palchen. He thinks he will ask Aba about these things. Besides, it is nearly noon and he wants to see if the fair is ready yet.

Climbing back up to Pemayangtse, Tashi passes groups of Buddhist pilgrims. Many have walked for days and even weeks along mountain trails to reach the monastery. On the porch of the temple, Tashi sees an old man and woman looking at the paintings of the Kings of the Four Quarters. He can tell from their dress that they come from Bhutan, a country to the east of India.

Behind the temple the fair is beginning. The smells of woodsmoke and spicy food cooking mingle in the mountain air. There is a great bustle of people. Merchants are hammering as they put up their stalls and shout directions to each other. Women sit on the

57

A Buddhist nun and a monk from Bhutan, a country next to India.

stone walls nursing their babies. Others squat, chatting together, in front of the wares they are selling. Children run about eating popped rice and peanuts. Toddlers suck on stalks of sugarcane.

For the hard-working Himalayan people who live in remote villages, festivals at monasteries give them a chance to meet and exchange information. Merchants carry up the hills the newest goods from factories in India, China, Taiwan, and Korea. At the Pemayangtse fair there are little transistor radios, green or purple plastic shoes, and Thermos bottles of every color. And always, there are many games to play.

When there is a break in the prayers, the novices rush down the stairs and around the back of the temple to the fairground. Before Tashi finds Samdup, his eyes light on a shiny game board lacquered with beautiful designs in green, blue, red, and black. He stops to admire it and the stall keeper says, "Come, try your luck." He gives Tashi some dice to roll in a cup. But when Tashi turns the cup upside down, his dice land on the wrong numbers and he loses his money.

When Tashi tells Samdup that all the money Aba gave him for the fair is now gone, Samdup says "Too bad." But Tashi feels as if Samdup doesn't really care. Samdup just talks about what he has to do for the Black Hat Dances tomorrow. A small demon of jealousy begins to grow in Tashi.

The fair behind the temple.

Tashi tries his luck at a gaming table.

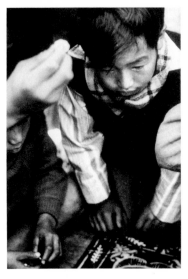

Losing is hard.

Masked dancers circle an enormous prayer flag at Pemayangtse.

6

 THE BLACK HAT DANCES AT PEMAYANGTSE

All Buddhist festivals are joyful and exciting events, but Samdup and Tashi like the festival at Pemayangtse with the Black Hat Dances best. The dances are performed each year at the monastery. They tell the story of the eternal struggle between good and evil forces.

An image of a demon, molded of barley flour and hidden under a black cloth, represents the forces of ignorance and evil. Every year the monks must destroy this evil to purify the world. First they do the Lama Dances. Carrying drums and cymbals, they whirl around a great circle in front of the temple. An enormous prayer flag stands in the center of the circle. Tashi sits on the grassy bank with the crowd of spectators watching the dances. From the temple comes the sounds of bells ringing, cymbals crashing, trumpets blasting, drums thundering, and through it all the steady, powerful chanting of the monks.

63

Tashi and the crowd of old and young people watch intently as the religious dances begin.

Samdup and Tashi know how hard it is to drive away evil. Even though they are sure the monks will succeed, they feel the tension of the struggle as they watch the dances. Buddhists believe this struggle between the forces of good and the forces of evil goes on within each individual. Festivals like the Black Hat Dances help people understand the power of evil and the recurrent need to be cleansed of it.

The Rinpoche and the monks who play the musical instruments for the dances sit in a special stand at the side of the circle. Samdup scurries back and forth bringing tea for them to drink out of beautiful teacups with silver lids.

But the festival is not all solemn. When the Rinpoche takes a break between dances and leaves his stand, the novices run to the tea stalls behind the temple to buy sweets. "Let's get some firecrackers, too," says Samdup. When they go back to the courtyard, Samdup tosses a firecracker toward the Rinpoche's stand. It explodes with a bang. The novices jump and yell. A dancer wearing a fierce demon mask leaps toward them waving his arms. The novices scatter and run. But in other corners of the courtyard they throw more firecrackers.

Tashi and a crowd of boys and girls peer in the side door of the temple. They smell a mixture of incense and paint. Suddenly a young monk dressed as a white-masked clown leaps out. With a bloodcurdling cry he chases the boys and girls back to the courtyard. More young monks dressed as clowns come cavorting after him. They do cartwheels and somersaults and run around the circle sprinkling white powder on everyone's head. The little girls squeal and cover their heads with their shawls.

At the boom of a drum a dozen dancers with huge wooden animal masks come dancing into the circle. There is a grinning tiger and a big bird with a wicked beak.

65

The Rinpoche and other high-ranking monks sit at a special stand. The novices wait to serve them.

Throwing firecrackers.

Then a blast of trumpets silences the crowd. Tashi cracks his knuckles in excitement. The powerful lama who is the chief Black Hat dancer appears on the temple porch. He is wearing a magnificent brocade gown. His huge black hat is topped by two cutout silver dragons with their tongues flicked out. The lama sits on a chair covered by a leopard skin. Tashi sees Samdup standing right beside this powerful lama. The demon of jealousy flicks again at Tashi's heart. He would like to be standing there like Samdup.

Slowly the venerable old lama descends the steps. Assisted by the novices, he begins the ancient ritual. Then, to the drone of horns and the slow, solemn beat of drums, he commences the mystic dance. The crowd watches spellbound. The lama whirls and whirls, round and round, leaping higher and higher. As he ends the first part of the dance, the elderly lama, exhausted by his efforts, crumbles and sinks like a leaf dropped by the wind. Two monks catch him. The crowd moans. The monks help the old lama into the temple, while the other dancers circle the demon effigy where the evil is encased.

Everyone waits anxiously until the lama reappears with his bell and dagger. It is only because of his great knowledge and practice of ancient rituals, and his limitless compassion, that the lama in the Black Hat Dances has the power to destroy the forces of evil. With a flash of the iron dagger the effigy is cut. The evil of the world is destroyed. Tashi heaves a great sigh of relief. He still wishes he were playing a part in the ceremonies like Samdup, but a flood of good feeling fills his heart.

Then the lama calls for the deer-headed dancer. He jumps into the circle. His silk robe shimmers blue and scarlet. The lama orders him to chop up the effigy and distribute it to the dancers in their ferocious masks. Then they all spin around the circle with their magnificent gowns billowing in the wind.

Samdup keeps his eyes on the powerful lama, with his tall hat and upturned shoes, sitting on a leopard skin.

It takes a steady hand to pour without spilling.

The lama begins his Black Hat Dance.

The powerful lama pulls out a black cloth. Flicking it, he beckons all the spirits of evil to enter the image which will be destroyed.

A deer-headed dancer bounds down the temple stairs.

The dances end. Everyone stands up. People cheer. They chat happily with each other. Tashi pushes through the crowd looking for his friend Samdup.

Merchants are taking down their stalls. The fairground is littered with orange peels and scraps of sugarcane. In a group of novices playing a last game of darts, Tashi spots Samdup. "Can you come play *koppe* tomorrow?" he asks him.

Samdup holds up his empty hands. "Yes," he laughs. "If you can give me some coins to toss." Tashi laughs too. "The lama knows what is mine is yours," he answers.

7

 A WALK IN THE WOODS

Samdup and Tashi have been taught a deep reverence for the world they live in. They have grown up feeling closely linked to all of nature, to the mountains around them, to plants and trees, animals and insects, and every other form of life. Buddhists believe that people should always keep in mind, whatever they are doing, a respect and compassion for the earth and all its creatures.

The day after the festival at Pemayangtse, Samdup and Tashi walk into the woods just below the monastery. A thick bed of brown leaves crackles under their bare feet and clouds of butterflies cross their path. Jade green moss drips from the tall trees. Before long they hear the sound of running water and come upon a sunlit glade. And its edge, nearly hidden by the deep forest, is a hugh white *chöten*.

Samdup and Tashi walk into the woods.

A *chöten* is a Buddhist religious monument filled with holy objects. Its shape is a reminder of the five basic elements of the universe: earth, water, fire, air, and ether. The square base represents the earth, the next level water, then fire, then air, and the orb at the very top represents the ether or the upper regions of space.

Samdup and Tashi circle the *chöten* clockwise three times, repeating *Om Mani Padme Hum.* The only sounds around them are birds chirping in the dense trees. But from afar they can hear, faintly, the heavy beat of rock music from a radio in he bazaar below. Tashi does not understand this music, but he likes to hear it and it makes him wonder about faraway places. "Listen," he says.

"I know nothing about such music," Samdup answers softly.

Both boys feel very peaceful in the forest by the *chöten.* But they know that life in the Himalayas will not remain as simple and quiet as it is now. More people are coming to these mountain regions. More roads are being built. More things to buy are appearing in the markets.

They climb higher up the hill and come to a cleared space on a small, flat summit. Behind a tumbled-down stone wall are ruins of an old palace and the houses around it. Weeds are growing in the roofless rooms. Tashi scrambles through an opening where a door once hung. It seems strange to him to think that once there were people living here.

"All things change but our faith lasts," says Samdup.

"That is true," Tashi answers. He knows, then, that whatever happens to him, he will always have his religion, just like Samdup. The demon feelings of jealousy flee from his heart.

Samdup looks down at his friend in the doorway. "My teacher told me," Samdup says, "that the Buddha taught, 'The man who talks much of his teaching but does not practice it himself is like a cowman counting another's cattle.' "

The boys come to a large Buddhist *chöten*.

While Samdup watches, Tashi steps through the doorway of a ruined house on a high, flat summit.

Climbing down through dense brush, Tashi and Samdup see three ancient stone *chötens*.

"You will be a good monk," Tashi smiles. Now he understands how different he is from Samdup.

The two boys walk to the edge of the summit. The hill is so high they feel as if they could reach out to touch the snowy peaks of Kanchenjunga. They look down. A sudden puff of wind blows away a cloud below them. There on a narrow ledge are three stone *chötens*. "The guardian deities," says Samdup.

White prayer flags on a ring of thin bamboo poles snap in the high clear air. "I must hurry back to Pemayangtse," Samdup whispers.

Tashi looks up at the rim of mountains darkening against the pale blue sky and wonders what lies beyond them. Then he tugs Samdup's sleeve. "If we run, we will have time for one more game of *koppe*."

"Whoever gets to the *Gonpa* first can flip the first coin," Samdup laughs. He races down the path ahead of Tashi.

The sun is beginning to slip behind the peaks of Kanchenjunga as the two laughing friends run down the leafy path. Their laughter rises from the darkening woods. It floats upward where—according to an old Sikkimese legend—joyous laughter, when it reaches the sky, freezes into shining stars.

Prayer flags pointing to the sky.

SELECTED BOOKS FOR FURTHER READING

Bancroft, Ann. *The Buddhist World*. Morristown, N.J.: Silver Burdett Co., 1984.

David-Neel, Alexandra. *Buddhism: Its Doctrines and Methods*. New York: St. Martin's Press, 1978.

Evans, Charles. *Kangchenjunga: The Untrodden Peak*. New York: E.P. Dutton & Co., 1957.

Fields, Rick. *How the Swans Came to the Lake: A Narrative History of Buddhism in America*. Boulder: Shambala, 1981.

Gyatso, Tenzin, The Fourteenth Dalai Lama. *Opening the Mind and Generating a Good Heart*. Dharamsala, India: Library of Tibetan Works and Archives, 1985.

83

His Holiness, The Dalai Lama of Tibet. *My Land and My People.* New York: McGraw-Hill Book Co., Inc., 1962.

Landaw, Jonathan. *Prince Siddhartha: The Story of Buddha.* London: Wisdom Publications, 1984.

Merton, Thomas. *The Asian Journal of Thomas Merton.* New York: New Directions, 1973.

INDEX